AVOCADO

THE GOODNESS OF
AVOCADO

40 DELICIOUS HEALTH-BOOSTING RECIPES

LUCY JESSOP

PHOTOGRAPHY BY CLARE WINFIELD

KYLE BOOKS

CONTENTS

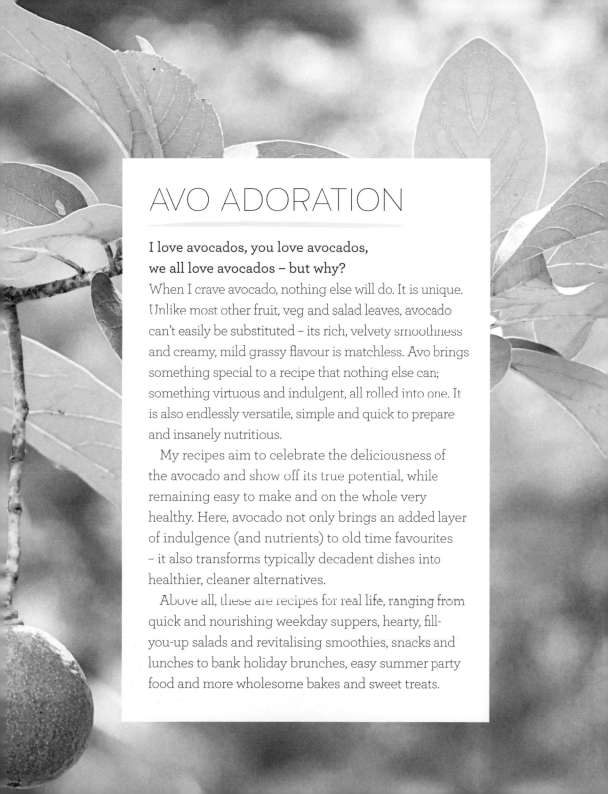

AVO ADORATION

I love avocados, you love avocados,
we all love avocados – but why?

When I crave avocado, nothing else will do. It is unique.
Unlike most other fruit, veg and salad leaves, avocado
can't easily be substituted – its rich, velvety smoothness
and creamy, mild grassy flavour is matchless. Avo brings
something special to a recipe that nothing else can;
something virtuous and indulgent, all rolled into one. It
is also endlessly versatile, simple and quick to prepare
and insanely nutritious.

My recipes aim to celebrate the deliciousness of
the avocado and show off its true potential, while
remaining easy to make and on the whole very
healthy. Here, avocado not only brings an added layer
of indulgence (and nutrients) to old time favourites
– it also transforms typically decadent dishes into
healthier, cleaner alternatives.

Above all, these are recipes for real life, ranging from
quick and nourishing weekday suppers, hearty, fill-
you-up salads and revitalising smoothies, snacks and
lunches to bank holiday brunches, easy summer party
food and more wholesome bakes and sweet treats.

WONDROUS WAYS

With avocados there are no rules; it really is the most versatile ingredient I've ever cooked with, for both flavour and the many wondrous ways it can be prepared. Mashed, whizzed, sliced, baked, griddled, frozen, you name it, the avocado shines in all these glorious guises. These recipes are divided into four chapters – based on the way you want to prepare your avocado: blitzed, smashed, chopped and sweet.

In the **Blitzed** chapter you'll find silky smooth salad dressings and soups, addictive pesto, luscious dips for dunking crunchy crudités or sweet potato chips, and nutritious smoothies.

The **Smashed** chapter brings you the classic guacamole plus twists to slather on toast, top with eggs, or scoop up with pitta or flatbread.

Avocados are diced and sliced as well as pickled, griddled and battered in the **Chopped** chapter – there are salsas, mouth-watering ceviches and summery suppers to boot.

Finally, the **Sweet** chapter reveals the surprising potential of the avocado, showing how it can replace butter, cream and even eggs to make delicious yet healthier bakes and puds.

If there are countless ways to prepare avocado, there is even more scope with flavour in play. Distinctive in its velvety texture, yet rich, creamy, mild and mellow in flavour, it is amazingly adaptable. Avocado calms and soothes where there's heat from chilli or fiery ginger, it balances zingy citrus and aromatic herbs, welcomes delicate spices, stands up to smoked fish or salty cheese, and its green, grassy, earthiness pairs seamlessly with all manner of vegetables, nuts, grains and seeds.

With every country enjoying its own delicious way of devouring avocado, these recipes are inspired by global flavours, taking their cue all the way from the avo's native Central America to Japan, the Middle East, Thailand, Spain, France, Italy, Scandinavia and more.

ALL ABOUT THE AVO

The avocado tree is native to Central America and Mexico and has been grown there and in South America for thousands of years. There are hundreds of varieties of avocado, but today only a handful of these are farmed for commercial export – they're grown everywhere from Mexico, Chile and Peru to California, South Africa and New Zealand.

Common varieties range from the pear shaped, smooth, green-skinned Fuerte, to rounder fruits such as the Reed and the popular pebbly skinned Hass. Others come in varying shapes and sizes – look out for Bacon, Lamb Hass, Pinkerton, Gwen and Zutano.

A NOTE ON HEALTHY EATING

For me, flavour is the only answer to healthy eating and is always top of my list when I create a recipe. With bags of flavour comes satisfaction, which leaves little need (or room) for anything too unhealthy.

None of these recipes have been shoe horned in for the sake of being healthy. Quite a few happen to be vegetarian, or are easily adapted to be so, and a good number are suitable for those avoiding gluten and dairy. Avocado equals goodness, therefore each recipe is by default nourishing and balanced. Many are naturally virtuous, being based on fresh vegetables, wholegrains and few processed ingredients, most of them are extremely good for you and one or two are once in a while treats to be savoured.

Mashed on toast with a pinch of sea salt and a squeeze of lime – it's the sense of luxury avocado brings to even the simplest of dishes which makes healthy eating a delight not a chore and the reason so many of us love avo. And I hope that's what all of the recipes in this book are – food to brighten your day while making you feel good, recipes you'll make over and over, share with family and pass onto friends. I hope you'll enjoy them as much as I have loved creating them.

NUTRITION
IN A NUTSHELL

The term 'superfood' is often overused, but for the avocado it's a deserved and well earned title. Avocados provide nearly 20 vitamins and minerals, including noteworthy amounts of fibre, good fats, folic acid, vitamin E and potassium.

There's no denying avocados are high in fat (and therefore calories), but that shouldn't put you off, because it's the good kind, monounsaturated fat, which has been found to help lower cholesterol levels and maintain a healthy weight. This sort of fat also improves the absorption of fat soluble vitamins A, D, E and K. In baking and desserts, avocado can offer a healthier alternative to butter or cream, which omits the need for dairy (therefore suitable for those who are intolerant) and also instantly cuts the overall saturated fat level.

◆ Vitamin E is a powerful antioxidant, which can help reduce the risk of chronic health conditions, such as heart disease, and protect the body's cells against damaging free radicals – overall it's important for keeping skin, eyes and the immune system healthy.

◆ Avocado is also a useful source of potassium (containing even more than bananas), which helps to balance sodium in the diet and maintain healthy blood pressure.
◆ Folic acid is another of avocado's vitamins. This vitamin (B9) is key to maintaining the healthy production of red blood cells and is especially important for women in the early stages of pregnancy or trying to conceive.

How to choose and store
◆ Choose an avocado that feels heavy for its size.
◆ Check it isn't bruised, damaged or squashed.
◆ Store at room temperature or in a cool place.

How to check for ripeness
◆ Hass avocado is green when unripe and blackens as it ripens; it should be dark brown, with a slightly purple hue when ripe.
◆ Don't use the colour of the skin alone to determine ripeness – the feel is equally, if not more, important. Hold the avocado in the palm of your hand and gently squeeze; it should yield just a little. Never firmly press, squeeze or prod an avo as it bruises easily.

How to ripen a rock hard avocado
Avocado (along with banana) releases ethylene gas, which is key to the ripening process. So place your unripe, hard avocado in a brown paper bag (or other container – an empty bread bin or cake tin works well). This will trap the ethylene gas and help it ripen more quickly. Store at room temperature.

Add a banana to the bag or tin, this will increase the amount of ethylene gas and speed up the process.

BLITZED

GREEN GAZPACHO SHOTS *DAIRY-FREE

On a scorching summer's day, a refreshing chilled soup can be soothing. This recipe takes its cue from Spanish gazpacho but leans towards vibrant Asian flavours. It looks stunning served in small shot glasses as a canapé. A summer party classic.

Serves 12 (50ml shots) as a canapé or 6–8 as a starter

1 garlic clove
½ cucumber (200g)
½ green pepper, deseeded
  and roughly chopped
25g blanched almonds
1 green chilli, deseeded
1 medium ripe avocado
  (about 150g flesh)
50g (1 thick slice) stale
  country style bread
A large handful of
  coriander leaves
A large handful of basil leaves
3 spring onions, white
  part only
3 tablespoons lime juice
250ml chilled water
Sea salt and freshly
  ground black pepper

For the crab and mango salsa
75g ripe mango flesh,
  finely diced
75g white crab meat
½ green chilli, deseeded
  and finely chopped
1 tablespoon finely chopped
  coriander leaves
Juice and zest of 1 lime

1. In a food-processor or blender whizz everything together (except the salsa) with a good pinch of sea salt and grind of black pepper until smooth. Add more water if needed to make a liquid consistency. Add more lime juice and seasoning to taste. Refrigerate for at least two hours or until very cold.

2. To serve, toss the diced mango with the crab, chilli, chopped coriander leaves, lime juice and zest. Pour the soup into shot glasses, over ice if it's a warm day, and top with the crab and mango mixture. Serve straight away.

Before preparing, always rinse an unpeeled avocado under cold running water to remove any dirt, then dry thoroughly using a clean tea-towel or kitchen paper.

THAI SWEETCORN & COCONUT SOUP

*DAIRY-FREE

Full of fragrant Thai flavours, avocado enriches this soup to make it a hearty, satisfying dish. Add shredded chicken for a more substantial meal. Use vegetable stock and omit the Thai fish sauce to make this vegetarian – use a little light soy sauce instead. To make it gluten-free, use gluten-free stock and tamari instead of fish sauce.

Serves 4

2 garlic cloves
2 red bird's eye chilli, deseeded if less heat preferred (reserve some)
4 kaffir lime leaves
2 echalion shallots
4 lemongrass stalks, roughly chopped
A small bunch each of basil and coriander, leaves and stalks chopped separately
1 × 400ml can coconut milk
800ml chicken or vegetable stock
2 tablespoons Thai fish sauce
4 fresh sweetcorn cobs
2 limes, plus lime wedges to serve
1 medium ripe avocado, plus extra to serve
Sea salt and freshly ground black pepper

1. Place the garlic, chilli, lime leaves, shallots and lemongrass into a food-processor, adding the basil and coriander stalks (about 1 tablespoon of each) and a splash of cold water before whizzing to a fine paste. Add to a large saucepan with a splash of water and cook, stirring, for 4–5 minutes until softened.

2. Add the coconut milk, stock and fish sauce and bring to the boil, reduce the heat and simmer for 20 minutes. Transfer to a liquidiser in batches, or use a stick blender and whizz until thick. Pass through a fine sieve, pressing the paste to extract as much flavour as possible.

3. Return the broth to the pan and bring back to a simmer. Cut the sweetcorn kernels away from the cobs and add them to the pan. Cook for about 10–12 minutes until tender.

4. Add the juice and zest of 1 lime and half of the basil and coriander leaves. Blitz half the soup in batches, with the avocado, until smooth. Return to the pan, and stir to combine with the rest of the soup.

5. Add most of the remaining herbs (reserving a little for garnish), seasoning and more lime juice to taste, then gently reheat.

6. Serve in bowls, scattered with some diced avocado, chopped chilli, and remaining coriander and basil leaves, torn. Add lime wedges on the side.

ROASTED GARLIC 'AVIOLI' *VEGETARIAN *GLUTEN-FREE

A truly punchy aioli is sometimes the only thing you need for dunking roasted potatoes, chips or a pile of crunchy vegetables. This version uses a gorgeous combination of avocado, Greek yogurt and roasted garlic for a lovely mellow flavour.

Serves 4–6

For the avioli
6 garlic cloves, unpeeled
Juice and zest of ½ lemon
2 tablespoons Greek style yogurt
1 small ripe avocado
Sea salt and freshly ground black pepper

To serve
A mixed selection of crudités e.g. radishes, baby carrots, cauliflower florets, celery

1. Preheat the oven to 180°C/ fan 160°C/gas mark 4. Place the garlic cloves on a piece of foil, add 1 tablespoon of water and wrap up to make a parcel. Bake for 30–40 minutes until the garlic is soft. Carefully unwrap (beware of the hot steam) and leave to cool slightly. Then squeeze the soft garlic from the skins into a food-processor.

2. Add the lemon juice and zest, yogurt and avocado flesh. Season generously and whizz until smooth. Add more seasoning or lemon juice to taste.

3. Spoon into a bowl and place on a board or platter with piles of raw vegetables for dipping.

Cutting down on saturated fat or dodging dairy? Swap traditional butter for avocado 'butter' by simply whizzing avocado with a squeeze of lime, pinch of sea salt and pinch of cayenne or paprika. Delicious on toast or as a sandwich spread

AVO 'CAESAR' SALAD

A well-made Caesar salad is hard to beat on a summer's day – crisp salad leaves lightly coated in an ever-so-moreish creamy, tangy dressing. The classic recipe uses raw egg yolks and plenty of extra virgin olive oil to create creaminess, but cheats' versions often use shop-bought mayonnaise. I've used avocado instead to make it super quick and easy, a little bit healthier and even more addictive. Top with chicken, if you like.

Serves 4

For the avo 'Caesar' dressing
1 small garlic clove,
    finely chopped
3 anchovies in oil,
    drained and chopped
1 heaped teaspoon Dijon
    mustard
4 tablespoons lemon juice
    (from 1–2 lemons)
25g Parmesan, finely grated
½ large ripe avocado
Sea salt and freshly
    ground black pepper

For the salad
1–2 baby gem or cos lettuce,
    cut into thin wedges
10 marinated anchovy fillets
1 avocado, sliced
A large handful of
    homemade croutons
    (see tip)
Parmesan shavings

1. Start with the dressing. In a food-processor, whizz the chopped garlic, anchovies, mustard, lemon juice and Parmesan until smooth. Roughly chop the avocado flesh and add to the food-processor. Blitz until smooth and add 2–3 tablespoons of chilled water if the dressing needs loosening – you want it to be a 'drizzleable' consistency. Season to taste with salt, pepper and a little more lemon juice.

2. For the salad, toss the lettuce leaves and anchovy fillets in a large bowl. Drizzle with just enough of the dressing to coat the leaves and toss together.

3. Divide between plates, add the sliced avocado, scatter over the homemade croutons and finish with freshly shaved Parmesan.

To make croutons, toss torn cubes of stale white bread in a little oil and plenty of seasoning, bake in a preheated oven at 200°C/fan 180°C/gas mark 6 for 5–10 minutes until golden and crisp.

TUNA SUSHI SALAD &
WASABI AVOCADO

*DAIRY-FREE

Everything that's great about sushi in a salad. It's good for you, filling, fresh and bursting with flavour. I make this punchy dressing on a weekly basis! Swap the seared tuna for cooked prawns if you prefer. To make this gluten-free, use tamari instead of soy sauce. Vegetarians can serve this with panfried mushrooms or tofu instead of tuna.

Serves 2

For the avo wasabi dressing
½ small ripe avocado
½ teaspoon wasabi paste
3 tablespoons lime juice
1 teaspoon toasted sesame oil
2 teaspoons soy sauce
2 teaspoons yuzu (optional)
Sea salt and freshly
  ground black pepper

For the salad
100g frozen edamame beans
250g cooked brown rice (or a
  mix of brown and wild rice)
100g sugarsnap peas, sliced
1 tablespoon pickled ginger,
  drained and shredded
½ small ripe avocado, sliced
75g radishes, finely sliced
4 spring onions, finely sliced
1 tablespoon each black
  and white sesame seeds
250g tuna steak
½ sheet of sushi nori, snipped
  into pieces (optional)

1. First make the dressing. Roughly chop the avocado flesh and add to a small food-processor with the remaining dressing ingredients. Whizz until smooth. Season to taste. Add 1 tablespoon of chilled water if the dressing needs loosening.

2. For the salad, cook the edamame beans in boiling, salted water for 2 minutes then drain and refresh under cold water. Add the beans to a large bowl along with the rice, sliced sugar snaps, pickled ginger, sliced avocado, radishes and spring onions. Add the dressing and gently toss together.

3. Spread the sesame seeds out on a plate. Preheat a frying pan until hot. Press the tuna into the seeds and turn to coat evenly on both sides. Sear the tuna for 30 seconds–1 minute on each side (depending on how thick it is – you want it to be rare). Transfer to a board and thinly slice.

4. Divide the salad between two plates. Top with the sliced tuna. Sprinkle with any remaining seeds and Nori pieces, if using.

SPIRALISED SALAD & AVO SATAY DRESSING

*VEGETARIAN *DAIRY-FREE

When you're after something light yet satisfying, this satay style dressing breathes a little life into spiralised vegetables. To make this recipe gluten-free, swap the soy sauce for tamari.

Serves 4

For the dressing
1 tablespoon soy sauce
1 heaped tablespoon
   freshly grated root ginger
2 tablespoons coconut milk
3 tablespoons good quality,
   crunchy peanut butter
½ teaspoon clear honey
4 tablespoons lime juice
zest of 1 lime
½ large ripe avocado
   (about 100g flesh)
2 red chillis, deseeded
   and finely chopped

For the spiralised salad
4 courgettes
2 large carrots
A small handful of
   coriander leaves

1. Put the soy, ginger, coconut milk and peanut butter, honey and lime juice into a small food-processor and whizz to a paste.

2. Add the lime zest and avocado flesh. Whizz until smooth. Taste to check the seasoning and add a little more soy and honey, if needed. Stir in most of the chilli.

3. Spiralise the vegetables (or grate if you don't have a spiraliser) and transfer to a large bowl. Add the dressing, most of the coriander leaves and toss together to coat. Divide between four plates, finish with the remaining chilli and coriander. Serve immediately.

If you have leftover ripe avocado, you can use it for baking – try the Squidgy Chocolate and Hazelnut Brownies on page 86 or the Banana and Walnut Bread on page 89.

AVOCADO 'PESTO' WITH LINGUINE

This has to be one of my absolute favourite ways with avocado. Its creamy texture works brilliantly as a substitute for olive oil in classic pesto and this spring twist combines savoury pistachios with uplifting mint and nutty Parmesan, making a pile of linguine far too easy to demolish. To make this recipe vegetarian, use vegetarian hard cheese.

Serves 2

150g linguine
100g frozen peas
1 courgette, coarsely grated

For the avo 'pesto'
50g pistachio kernels
½ garlic clove, finely chopped
1 medium ripe avocado
Juice of ½ lemon, plus
   extra wedges to serve
50g Pecorino or Parmesan
   cheese, finely grated,
   plus extra to serve
40g picked mint leaves,
   plus extra to serve
Sea salt and freshly ground
   black pepper

1. Preheat the oven to 200°C/ fan 180°C/gas mark 6. First make the pesto. Spread the pistachios out on a large baking tray. Bake in the oven for 4–5 minutes until toasted. Leave to cool.

2. Add the cooled nuts to a food-processor along with the garlic. Roughly chop the avocado flesh. Add this to the food-processor, along with the lemon juice, grated cheese and mint leaves and 2 tablespoons of cold water.

3. Add a good pinch of salt and pepper. Pulse to make a chunky, pesto-like consistency – add a little more water, if needed, or lemon juice to taste.

4. Next cook the pasta in boiling, salted water until al dente. Add the peas to the pan for the last minute of cooking time.

5. Drain well, reserving a couple of tablespoons of the cooking water and return to the pan. Add the grated courgette and pesto, along with the reserved water to loosen. Toss together. Serve with grated cheese and mint leaves.

SWEET POTATO CHIPS & AVOCADO 'MAYO'

*VEGETARIAN *DAIRY-FREE *GLUTEN-FREE

You may never return to regular mayonnaise again. This unintentionally dairy and egg free 'mayo' is made simply from silky smooth avocados, fiery ginger, a teensy bit of garlic and zippy limes, with an optional extra kick from chilli. Slather it into a steak sandwich or dollop on the side of these addictive sweet potato chips.

Serves 4

For the sweet potato chips
4 sweet potatoes
  (about 800g)
3 tablespoons olive oil
3 tablespoons polenta
1 teaspoon paprika
Sea salt

For the 'mayo'
1 large ripe avocado
40g root ginger, peeled
  and finely grated
½ small garlic clove, crushed
3 tablespoons lime juice
Zest of 1 lime
Dash of Tabasco (optional)
1 tablespoon olive oil

1. Preheat the oven to 200°C/ fan 180°C/gas mark 6. Wash the sweet potatoes in cold water and dry thoroughly with a clean tea-towel – there's no need to peel them. Then cut lengthways into long 1cm wide chips. Transfer to a large bowl. Add the oil and toss to coat. Then add the polenta, paprika and a good pinch of salt. Mix well to evenly coat.

2. Spread the chips between two large roasting tins. They need as much space as possible, so should be in a single layer. Bake for 35–40 minutes until tender and crisp.

3. Meanwhile, make the 'mayo' dip. Place the avocado flesh in a food-processor. Add the grated ginger, garlic, lime juice and zest, Tabasco (if using), olive oil, 1 tablespoon of cold water and a large pinch of salt. Whizz until smooth. Transfer to a small dish and serve with the warm, crunchy sweet potato chips.

Smoothies provide a big whack of nutrients in one speedy hit. Avocados add velvety smoothness and eliminate the need for dairy whilst boosting the goodness levels even further. All of these smoothies are best made with chilled (or frozen) fruit.

SMOOTHIES

ALL *VEGETARIAN *GLUTEN-FREE *DAIRY-FREE

All serve 2

THE BERRY ONE

½ large ripe avocado
100g frozen raspberries
  (or use fresh)
½ ripe banana
  (about 60g)
2 teaspoons clear honey
200ml chilled coconut
  water

Hydrating, energising, hunger quashing and utterly delicious, this smoothie is great any time of day, be it breakfast, post workout or just when you need a pick me up.

Add the avocado flesh to a high-speed blender, food-processor or liquidiser along with the other ingredients. Whizz until smooth. Pour into two glasses and serve straight away.

THE TROPICAL ONE

½ large ripe avocado
125g frozen or fresh
  mango flesh
Juice of ½ lime
250ml coconut milk
  (the drinking kind,
  not the canned variety)
½–1 teaspoon honey
  (depending on the
  sweetness of your mango)
2 passion fruit, seeds
  and pulp scooped out
  (optional)

Pretend you're basking in the sunshine on a beach with this smoothie and your day is bound to get off to a good start.

Add the avocado flesh to a high-speed blender, food-processor or liquidiser along with the remainder of the ingredients, except the passion fruit. Whizz until smooth. Stir in the passion fruit pulp and seeds, if you like. Pour into two glasses and serve straight away.

THE NUTTY ONE

½ large ripe avocado
1 ripe banana, peeled
200ml chilled unsweetened
  almond milk
1 tablespoon almond
  butter (or peanut butter)
1–2 teaspoons honey,
  to taste, depending
  on the ripeness of
  your banana
1 tablespoon oats (check
  they are gluten-free)

**This tastes much naughtier than it is, a little bit
like a banana milkshake. Perfect for a speedy
on-the-go breakfast or post exercise, this
smoothie will replenish those energy levels fast.**

Add the avocado flesh to a high-speed blender,
food-processor or liquidiser along with the remaining
ingredients. Whizz until smooth. Pour into two glasses
and serve straight away.

THE GREEN ONE

½ large ripe avocado
¼ ripe banana
25g spinach leaves
100g ripe melon
  (e.g. honeydew), cut
  into chunks
1 apple, quartered and core
  removed (about 100g)
A thumb sized piece of
  root ginger, peeled
  and grated
175ml chilled coconut water
10 mint leaves, to taste

**This glorious green smoothie packs in the vitamins.
Drink it for breakfast and feel all smug for the rest
of the day.**

Add the avocado flesh to a high-speed blender,
food-processor or liquidiser along with the other
ingredients. Whizz until smooth. Pour into two
glasses and serve straight away.

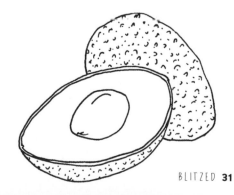

SMASHED

CLASSIC 'GUAC' WITH TORTILLA CHIPS

*VEGETARIAN

This popular favourite will never go out of fashion. And there are so many variations on this classic. Some are incredibly basic, combining just avocado, lime and salt, some use garlic instead of onion, or leave out tomatoes and coriander. Others are mouth tinglingly spicy, and the texture ranges from rough and ready to super smooth. This is my favourite version, but it's worth experimenting to find yours – the possibilities are endless.

Serves 4

For the tortillas
8 soft corn tortillas
2 tablespoons vegetable oil
1 teaspoon cumin seeds
1 teaspoon sea salt
1 teaspoon smoked paprika
Zest of 2 limes

For the guacamole
2 ripe avocados
1 red chilli, deseeded
   and finely chopped
75g cherry tomatoes,
   roughly chopped
Juice and zest of 1 lime
1 tablespoon finely
   chopped red onion
A small handful of coriander
   leaves, roughly chopped

1. First make the tortilla chips. Preheat the oven to 220°C/fan 200°C/gas mark 7. Lightly brush the tortillas with oil on both sides. Then cut each tortilla into eight triangles.

2. Put the cumin seeds into a pestle and mortar with ½ teaspoon of sea salt and lightly crush. Mix in the smoked paprika. Put half of the tortilla triangles into a bowl and add half of the spice mix. Toss gently with clean hands to coat. Spread out in a single layer on a large baking tray. Repeat with the rest of the tortillas. You will need at least three large baking trays for this (or bake in batches).

3. Bake in the oven for about 5 minutes until crisp and golden. Leave to cool slightly.

4. Meanwhile, make the guacamole. Roughly chop the avocado flesh, then transfer to a bowl along with the chopped chilli and tomatoes, lime juice and zest, red onion and coriander. Add a good pinch of sea salt, mix well and check the seasoning.

5. Mix the remaining ½ teaspoon of sea salt with the lime zest and sprinkle over the tortilla chips. Serve straight away with the guacamole.

GOOD-FOR-YOU 'GUAC' WITH PITTA CRISPS

*VEGETARIAN *DAIRY-FREE

As if guacamole needed any help on the health front. Yes, that's right, it's already good for you, but this version has added goodness from super nutritious kale, edamame and pumpkin seeds to make it a really healthy snack. Warning: fennel and chilli make these pittas dangerously moreish so you may need to operate some willpower. You can also make the pitta crisps with gluten-free pittas or serve with crudités.

Serves 4–6

For the fennel and chilli pitta crisps
3 wholemeal pitta breads
2 tablespoons olive oil
1½ teaspoon fennel seeds
½ teaspoon sea salt, plus extra for the guacamole
A large pinch dried chilli flakes

For the guacamole
100g frozen edamame beans
75g kale
1 small garlic clove, finely chopped
Juice and zest of 1 lemon
2 ripe avocados
1 tablespoon pumpkin seeds, toasted (optional)

1. First make the pitta crisps. Preheat the oven to 200°C/fan 180°C/gas mark 6. Cut the pittas in half horizontally, to make two thin layers from each one. Cut each of these into rough triangles. Spread out on two large baking trays and drizzle with the oil. Toss to coat. Crush the fennel seeds with the sea salt and chilli flakes and sprinkle evenly over the pitta triangles. Bake for about 8 minutes or until crisp.

2. For the guacamole, put the edamame and kale in a bowl and cover with boiling water. Set aside for 3 minutes, then drain and run under the cold tap. Drain thoroughly, then transfer to a food-processor to roughly chop, or do this by hand.

3. Put the garlic, lemon juice and zest into a bowl. Roughly chop the avocado flesh, mash with a fork, then add this to the bowl along with the kale and edamame (or add this to food-processor and pulse briefly to combine). Add a generous pinch of salt, to taste, and mix well. Sprinkle with toasted pumpkin seeds before serving with the pitta crisps.

SMOKEY AVOCADO, PEPPERS & CHORIZO

*DAIRY-FREE

There's no going back once you've tried this – it might well become a regular weekend brunch fixture.

Serves 2

1 small garlic clove
1 large ripe avocado
A good squeeze of lemon juice
A large pinch of smoked
  paprika
1 ready roasted pepper from
  a jar (about 60g), drained
  and finely chopped
Sea salt and freshly ground
  black pepper
125g cooking chorizo
  sausage, halved lengthways
2 slices sourdough bread
A large handful of spinach
  or rocket leaves

1. Finely chop the garlic. Roughly chop the avocado flesh and mix with the garlic. Add the lemon juice, smoked paprika and chopped peppers. Lightly mash with a fork. Add salt and pepper and more lemon juice to taste.

2. Now heat a griddle pan until hot and griddle the chorizo for about 5 minutes, turning halfway until cooked through.

3. Toast the sourdough bread (either in a toaster or using the griddle pan) and put onto individual plates. Spread each slice with a dollop of the smashed avocado, add a handful of leaves, and top with the chorizo. Serve straight away.

LEMONY AVO WITH ROCKET & TROUT *DAIRY-FREE

Spread on toasted rye bread and topped with hot smoked trout, this gorgeously peppery Italian twist on a guacamole makes a delicious lunch. Top with a poached egg for a filling weekend brunch. For a vegetarian option, a creamy cheese works really well – add torn mozzarella or a spoonful of ricotta.

Serves 2

1 large ripe avocado
Sea salt and freshly
   ground black pepper
Juice of ½ lemon
2 teaspoons extra virgin
   olive oil or avocado oil
25g rocket leaves
2 large slices of rye or
   wholewheat bread
125g hot-smoked trout
   or salmon
Lemon wedges, to serve

1. Roughly mash the avocado flesh on a clean board with a large pinch of sea salt and half of the lemon juice, then transfer to a bowl. Add 1 teaspoon of the olive oil or avocado oil and a generous grind of black pepper. Mix well. Roughly chop half of the rocket leaves and fold into the smashed avocado.

2. Toast the bread and arrange on two plates. Spoon the smashed avocado onto each slice of toast. Flake over the hot smoked fish. Toss the rest of the rocket leaves with the remaining olive oil and lemon juice and season. Serve alongside the toast with lemon wedges to squeeze over, if you like.

If your avocado is perfectly ripe in the morning and you plan to eat it later that evening, place it in the fridge to prevent it from overripening.

AVOCADO FATTOUSH
WITH FALAFEL *VEGETARIAN

Fattoush is a chopped salad with Lebanese roots, which combines zingy sumac and fragrant herbs with the fresh crunch of summer vegetables – strips of toasted pitta bread are added as a way of using them up. Smashing avocado with these flavours transforms this light salad into a sustaining and satisfying lunch. Make this dairy-free by leaving out the feta.

Serves 2

For the sumac spiced avocado
1 small garlic clove
Sea salt
1 tablespoon tahini paste
Juice of ½ lemon
1 large ripe avocado
A large pinch of sumac
50g cherry tomatoes,
   finely chopped
6 mint leaves, shredded,
   plus baby mint leaves
   to serve

To serve
2 wholemeal flatbreads
   or pitta breads, warmed
6 ready-made falafel,
   toasted or griddled
¼ cucumber, diced
50g cherry tomatoes,
   quartered
A handful of pitted
   Kalamata olives, halved
¼ red onion, finely sliced
50g feta cheese, crumbled
   (optional)

1. Crush the garlic in a pestle and mortar with a pinch of sea salt and twist of black pepper, then add to a bowl and stir in the tahini paste and lemon juice.

2. Scoop out the avocado flesh and roughly chop. Add to the bowl with the sumac, chopped tomatoes and shredded mint. Mix together until combined, and season to taste.

3. To serve, top a warm flatbread or pitta with a spoonful of the avocado mixture and some falafel, then scatter over cucumber, tomatoes, olives, red onion, and crumbled feta, if using.

AVOCADO WITH PEAS, MINT & FETA

*VEGETARIAN

Makes 12 crostini

Serves 4 as a starter

or 4–6 as canapés

Avocado adds a luxurious note to this classic spring creation. These are easy-peasy canapés, which are even easier to eat.

150g frozen peas

2 spring onions, white
part only, finely chopped

1 ripe avocado, flesh diced

1 heaped tablespoon finely
chopped mint leaves, plus
baby mint leaves to serve

1 tablespoon lemon juice
(about ½ lemon)

1 teaspoon extra virgin olive
oil or avocado oil, plus
extra to drizzle (optional)

Sea salt and freshly
ground black pepper

75g feta cheese

½ wholegrain or white
baguette, sliced into
12 × 1cm rounds

1. Preheat the grill to medium. Add the peas to a pan of boiling water, bring back to the boil, simmer for 1 minute, drain, and refresh in a bowl of cold water. Drain again, then set aside 2 tablespoons of the peas. Blitz the rest in a food-processor with the spring onions, half the avocado, chopped mint, lemon juice and olive oil to make a rough purée. Transfer to a bowl.

2. Add the remaining avocado, mix to combine, then season to taste with salt and pepper. Add more lemon juice if you prefer a sharper taste.

3. Now toast the baguette rounds under the preheated grill for about 1 minute, turning halfway. Once the toast has cooled a little, spoon some of the smashed mixture onto each one. Transfer to a board or serving platter, crumble over the feta, and top with mint leaves. Drizzle with extra virgin olive oil or avocado oil, if you like.

AVOCADO HUMMUS
& ROASTED DUKKAH

*VEGETARIAN *DAIRY-FREE

Who doesn't love hummus? It's a great go-to savoury snack when you need to surrender to those sudden hunger pangs and an instant, healthy energy boost. Avocado enriches this hummus and the hit of flavour from this easy Egyptian spice mix really livens it up. You can also sprinkle this versatile spice mix over pitta crisps or toss with vegetables before roasting.

Serves 4–6

For the roasted dukkah
1 tablespoon each blanched
   almonds and hazelnuts
2 teaspoons sesame seeds
1 teaspoon cumin seeds
½ teaspoon coriander seeds
½ teaspoon fennel seeds

For the hummus
1 garlic clove, finely chopped
1 tablespoon tahini paste
2 tablespoons lemon juice
   and zest of ½ lemon
Sea salt
400g can chickpeas, drained
1 ripe avocado
2 tablespoons chopped
   coriander

To serve
Warm flatbreads, cut
   into strips

1. Preheat the oven to 180°C/ fan 160°C/gas mark 4. First prepare the roasted dukkah. Spread the nuts out in a large roasting tin. Bake for 5 minutes, then scatter over the remaining seeds and spices. Roast for a further 2–3 minutes until fragrant. Do keep an eye on them as you don't want the spices to burn. Set aside to cool slightly. Then transfer to a pestle and mortar and lightly crush or coarsely grind in a food-processor.

2. Now make the hummus. Put the garlic in a food-processor with the tahini paste, lemon juice and zest and a large pinch of salt. Set aside a tablespoon of chickpeas and add the remainder to the food-processor along with 2 tablespoons of the spice mix and the avocado. Whizz to a chunky purée (you want to keep some of the texture).

3. Add the chopped coriander and mix well. Season to taste.

4. Spoon into a serving dish, top with the reserved chickpeas and sprinkle with a little more of the dukkah spices. Serve with warmed flatbreads to dip.

CHOPPED

AVO PRAWN COCKTAIL & CHARRED LETTUCE

*DAIRY-FREE

A timeless classic, this avo twist on the retro starter brings this favourite bang up to date.

Serves 2

1 baby gem lettuce, cut in
   half lengthways
Olive oil for brushing
200g cooked prawns
1 ripe avocado, diced
Cayenne pepper

For the Marie Rose sauce
100g good quality
   mayonnaise (about
   6 tablespoons)
1 tablespoon tomato ketchup
¼ teaspoon Tabasco sauce
Juice of ½ lemon, plus
   lemon wedges to serve
½ teaspoon Worcestershire
   sauce
Sea salt and freshly
   ground black pepper
1 tablespoon chopped chives

1. First make the Marie Rose sauce. In a bowl combine the mayonnaise, ketchup, Tabasco, lemon juice and Worcestershire sauce. Season to taste with a little sea salt and freshly ground pepper. Add a little more lemon juice if needed, then stir in half of the chopped chives.

2. Preheat a ridged griddle pan until very hot. Lightly brush the cut side of each lettuce half with a little oil and season. When the griddle pan is very hot, add the lettuce halves cut side down for 2 minutes until lines appear. Turn over and cook for a minute. Then transfer one lettuce half, cut side up, to each plate.

3. Add the prawns to the Marie Rose sauce and mix well. Toss the diced avocado with a squeeze of lemon juice and remaining chives. Top each lettuce half with some of the prawn cocktail, then spoon over the avocado. Sprinkle with a little cayenne pepper. Serve with lemon wedges on the side to squeeze over.

For those with good knife skills and more experienced cooks, you can use a knife to remove the stone. Hold the avocado in place and in one swift motion firmly lodge the length of a heavy, sharp knife into the surface of the stone – it should stay lodged there. Then hold the avocado and gently twist the knife to release the stone. Be careful here as avocado flesh is slippery.

AVO SALMON CEVICHE WITH TOSTADAS

*DAIRY-FREE

The perfect light bite for a balmy summer evening – zesty lime, fragrant coriander and a little kick from chilli make these dangerously addictive. Make sure your salmon is a fresh as possible.

Serves 2–3
Makes 6 mini tostadas

200g very fresh salmon,
  skinless and boneless
½ teaspoon sea salt
8 tablespoons lime juice
  (about 2–3 limes)
1 red chilli, deseeded and
  finely chopped
¼ small red onion, finely
  chopped
Vegetable oil, for frying
6 mini corn tortillas
  or 4 standard sized
  corn tortillas
Paprika, to sprinkle
1 ripe avocado
2 tablespoons chopped
  coriander

1. Cut the salmon into 1cm cubes as evenly as you can. Transfer to a bowl, add the salt, lime juice, chilli and red onion. Mix well and refrigerate for 10 minutes.

2. Meanwhile, make the tostadas. If you can get hold of mini corn tortillas, use these, if not buy the standard corn tortillas and use a 10cm circular cutter to cut out six smaller rounds. Use the trimmings to make tortilla chips. Pour enough oil into a frying pan to cover the base in a thin layer and heat until very hot. Carefully fry the tortillas in batches, for about 30 seconds on each side, and transfer to a plate lined with kitchen paper. Sprinkle with sea salt and a little paprika.

3. Dice the avocado flesh into 1cm cubes and transfer to a bowl. Strain the marinated salmon mixture of any excess lime juice and add to the bowl with the avocado, then add the coriander and gently toss together. Taste to check the seasoning.

4. Top each tostada with a spoonful of ceviche and eat straight away.

SWEETCORN FRITTERS & CHILLI-AVO SALSA
*VEGETARIAN

This sprightly salsa will perk up even the dreariest of winter mornings. Pile it onto these mouth-watering sweetcorn fritters – and top with a runny fried egg, if you like.

Serves 2–3 (makes 6 fritters)

For the salsa
1 ripe avocado
Juice and zest of 1 lime
125g cherry tomatoes, quartered
1 red chilli, deseeded and finely chopped
2 spring onions, finely sliced
2 tablespoons chopped coriander leaves
Sea salt

For the fritters
340g can sweetcorn, drained
1 large egg, beaten
3 tablespoons self-raising flour
2 tablespoons finely chopped chives
75g feta cheese or hard goat's cheese, cubed
Butter and vegetable oil for frying

To serve
Fried eggs (optional)

1. For the salsa, dice the avocado flesh and put in a large bowl. Add the lime juice and zest, mix well, then add the tomatoes, most of the chilli, spring onions, chopped coriander and a pinch of sea salt. Set aside.

2. Now make the fritters. Put half the sweetcorn, egg, flour, and a large pinch of salt into a food-processor. Whizz until smooth, then transfer to a bowl. Fold in the rest of the sweetcorn, chives and feta.

3. Heat the vegetable oil and butter in a large, non-stick frying pan. When hot, add spoonfuls of the mixture. You'll need about 3 tablespoons per fritter. Fry, in batches, over a medium heat for 2–3 minutes on each side until golden. You can keep them warm in a low oven while you cook the rest.

4. Stack two or three fritters onto each plate, add a spoonful of salsa and sprinkle with the reserved chilli. Top with a fried egg, if you like.

BOILED EGGS & CRISPY AVOCADO 'CHIPS'

These melt-in-the-mouth avocado chips bring a whole new dimension to boiled eggs. Crispy on the outside and beautifully buttery in the centre, they are just perfect for dipping into a hot, runny yolk. To make this recipe vegetarian use vegetarian hard cheese.

Serves 2

1 firm but ripe avocado,
    cut lengthways into
    1cm slices
4 tablespoons plain flour
¼ teaspoon paprika or
    cayenne pepper
½ teaspoon fine salt
3 eggs
50g Japanese-style
    panko breadcrumbs
25g finely grated
    Parmesan cheese or
    vegetarian hard cheese
Vegetable oil, for frying

1. Take three deep plates and place them next to each other. Put the flour, paprika or cayenne pepper and salt onto the first plate. Crack one egg onto the second plate and lightly whisk, then put the breadcrumbs, Parmesan and some seasoning onto the final plate and mix well.

2. Take a slice of avocado and gently toss in the flour to coat, then dip in the beaten egg and finally turn in the breadcrumb mixture until evenly coated. Repeat with the remaining slices.

3. Pour enough oil into a non-stick frying pan to cover the base. Set over a medium heat for a few minutes. When hot, add the crumbed avocado slices in batches and fry for 1–2 minutes each side until crisp and golden. Transfer to a plate lined with kitchen paper. If you're not sure if the oil is hot enough, test with a small piece of bread. The bread should sizzle on touching the oil and turn golden after a minute or so.

4. When the avocado is almost done. Put the remaining eggs into a pan of cold water. Bring to the boil, then set the timer and simmer for 3 minutes. Remove straight away and place in egg cups. Use a knife to slice away the top of each egg. Serve a few crispy avocado slices with the soft boiled eggs to dip in.

To cook the avocado chips with less fat, you can bake them on a tray lined with greaseproof paper in a preheated oven (220°C/fan 200°C/gas mark 7) for 10 minutes.

CRISPBREAD, MACKEREL & DILL PICKLED AVO

These homemade crispbreads are dead simple to make. If you're short of time you can find lots of good ready-made versions, or this would also work as a topping for toasted rye bread or a wholewheat bagel. The crispbreads will keep for a few days in an airtight container.

Serves 4
Makes 8–10 crispbreads
(approx. 15cm × 8cm
rectangles)

For the seeded crispbreads
100g rye flour
100g plain flour
100g wholemeal flour
1 teaspoon fine salt
150g mixed seeds
  (e.g. sesame, pumpkin,
  sunflower, linseed)
1 teaspoon caraway seeds
2 teaspoons clear honey
4 tablespoons olive oil
125ml water

For the avo and cucumber pickle
½ cucumber
½ teaspoon fine salt
2 tablespoons white
  wine vinegar
2 tablespoons lemon juice
  (plus the zest of 1 lemon)
1 tablespoon caster sugar
2 tablespoons chopped dill,
  plus a few sprigs to serve
1 firm but ripe avocado, sliced

cream cheese, to serve
250g smoked peppered
  mackerel, to serve

1. For the crispbreads, preheat the oven to 180°C/fan 160°C/gas mark 4. Mix together the flours, salt and 100g of the mixed seeds in a large bowl and add half the caraway seeds. In a jug whisk the honey and olive oil with the water. Make a well in the centre of the dry ingredients and pour in most of the liquid. Mix together to make a dough, adding the remainder of the liquid if needed to bring the dough together.

2. Knead briefly, then roll out the dough on a lightly floured surface to a large rectangle 3mm thick. Sprinkle with the remaining seeds and caraway seeds and lightly roll into the surface of the dough. Cut the dough into 6–8 rectangles. Transfer to two large baking trays lined with greaseproof paper. Gather up the dough trimmings and reroll to get some more. Bake for about 20 minutes until pale golden, then transfer to a cooling rack.

3. For the pickle, halve the cucumber lengthways, scrape out the seeds, then finely slice into half moons and place in a colander in the sink. Add the salt and toss to coat. Place a piece of greaseproof paper on top of the cucumber and weigh it down with something heavy – a can works well. Set aside for 15 minutes.

4. Meanwhile, put the vinegar, lemon juice and sugar in a small bowl, stir until the sugar dissolves. Then add half of the dill.

5. Rinse the cucumber of salt and dry between sheets of kitchen paper. Add to the pickling liquid with the avocado. Cover and refrigerate for 1 hour. Then strain, discarding the liquid, and toss with the remaining dill. Season.

6. Spread a little cream cheese onto a crispbread, top with the pickled avocado and cucumber and finish with flaked smoked mackerel. Add a few sprigs of dill.

AVO TUNA TARTARE & SESAME TOASTS *DAIRY-FREE

This savoury soy, sesame and ginger dressing goes so well with meaty tuna, and is balanced with the cooling crunch of cucumber and mellow avocado. A delicious topping for mouth-watering sesame toasts.

Serves 4 as a starter

1 large ripe but firm avocado, diced into 2cm cubes
½ cucumber, deseeded and chopped into 2cm cubes
275g fresh tuna steak, diced into 1cm cubes
2 spring onions, finely sliced
1 teaspoon sesame seeds, toasted, to serve

For the sesame toasts
1 thin white baguette (cut into 12 × 1cm slices)
1 tablespoon toasted sesame oil
4 teaspoons each white and black sesame seeds

For the dressing
1 tablespoon soy sauce
Juice of 2 limes, plus wedges
1 teaspoon toasted sesame oil
1 red chilli
1 tablespoon finely grated root ginger
1 tablespoon chopped coriander, plus a small handful of leaves

1. First make the dressing. Put the soy sauce, lime juice, sesame oil, half the chilli, ginger and chopped coriander into a food-processor. Whizz until smooth, then transfer to a bowl.

2. Now start the tartare. Place the diced avocado and cucumber into another bowl, add half the dressing and mix gently to combine.

3. Preheat the grill to high, ready for the sesame toasts. To make, spread the baguette slices out in a single layer on a baking tray. Grill until just toasted then remove from the grill, turn over and brush the untoasted side with the sesame oil. Spread the mixed sesame seeds evenly on top of the toasts, return to the grill for 30–60 seconds until toasted and golden.

4. Add the diced tuna and reserved coriander leaves to the bowl with the remaining dressing and toss together.

5. To serve, spoon a quarter of the avocado and cucumber mixture into an 8cm chef's ring (or use a biscuit cutter) on the centre of a plate and spread out evenly to fill the ring. Spoon the tuna tartare on top. Garnish with a little spring onion and a sprinkling of toasted sesame seeds. Repeat with the remaining three servings on individual plates. Serve with the sesame toasts on the side.

If you don't have a chef's ring you can also serve the tartare in small glasses.

PRAWN & AVOCADO SPRING ROLLS

Clean, fresh and fragrant – velvety smooth avocado and succulent, sweet prawns are a wonderful double act in this twist on this Vietnamese classic (photo overleaf).

Serves 4

80g rice noodles
8 rice paper wrappers
16 cooked large prawns
   (about 150g), peeled
   and halved horizontally
A small handful of
   coriander leaves
2–3 tablespoons finely
   shredded mint leaves,
   plus a few baby leaves
⅓ cucumber, deseeded and
   sliced into thin lengths
1 carrot, roughly grated
   or sliced into matchsticks
¼ iceberg lettuce, finely
   shredded
1 large ripe avocado,
   thinly sliced
3 tablespoons salted peanuts,
   roughly chopped

For the dipping sauce
Juice and zest of 2 limes
2 teaspoons light brown
   or palm sugar
2 tablespoons Thai fish sauce
1 tablespoon soy sauce
1 bird's eye chilli, deseeded
   and finely chopped

1. Put the rice noodles in a bowl and cover with boiling water. Leave for 4–5 minutes, drain well and run under cold water. Set aside.

2. Now fill a bowl with cold water. Briefly dip a rice paper wrapper into the water, shake off any excess and transfer to a clean chopping board. This should make them pliable. Be careful not to submerge for too long as they become delicate and tricky to handle.

3. Place four prawn halves in a line in the centre of a rice paper wrapper, then add a line of coriander and mint alongside. Top with a few rice noodles, a little cucumber, carrot, lettuce and avocado.

4. Add a sprinkle of peanuts. Then fold the bottom of the wrapper over the filling. Fold in the sides and roll up. Repeat with the remaining wrappers and filling.

5. For the dipping sauce, whisk the lime juice and zest with the sugar, fish and soy sauce. Then stir in the chilli. Add water to taste.

6. Serve the spring rolls with the dipping sauce and a sprinkling of coriander leaves.

SWEET POTATO HASH & SMOKEY FRIJOLES
*VEGETARIAN

Comforting sweet potato hash, smoky black beans and charred, buttery avocado make this a warming veggie supper. This dish can easily be made gluten-free – just use gluten-free vegetable stock.

Serves 4

800g sweet potato (about 4),
    cut into 3cm chunks
100g feta cheese, to serve
Lime wedges, to serve
4 eggs for frying

For the frijoles
2 teaspoons cumin seeds
1 tablespoon olive oil
1 red onion, finely chopped
2 garlic cloves, finely chopped
1 teaspoon dried oregano
1 teaspoon smoked paprika
400g can black beans, drained
250ml hot vegetable stock
Sea salt and freshly
    ground black pepper

For the hash
¼ teaspoon dried chilli flakes
    or 1 red chilli, deseeded
    and finely chopped
1 garlic clove, crushed
4 spring onions, finely sliced
25g coriander, stalks and
    leaves chopped separately
1–2 tablespoons oil
2 firm but ripe avocados

1. Place the sweet potatoes in a microwave-proof bowl. Cover and microwave at 600W for 10 minutes or until completely tender (alternatively, steam or roast, covered, in the oven).

2. To make the frijoles, preheat a deep sauté or frying pan, add the cumin seeds and cook for about a minute until fragrant. Add the oil, onion and garlic and soften gently for 10 minutes. Add the oregano, smoked paprika, black beans and stock and slowly bring to a simmer. Cook gently for 15 minutes, stirring occasionally, then season to taste.

3. Roughly mash the cooked sweet potato with a fork, then mix in the chilli flakes or fresh chilli, crushed garlic, spring onions, chopped coriander stalks and some seasoning. Mix well. Heat a splash of oil in a large frying pan. Roughly divide the sweet potato mash

into four equal amounts. Add each spoonful to the pan and fry for 3–4 minutes until crispy and golden, flip over and cook for a further 2–3 minutes. Remove from the pan and keep warm. Return the pan to the heat, add a little more oil and fry the eggs to your liking.

4. Meanwhile, heat a ridged griddle pan until hot. Lightly brush the cut side of each avocado half with a little oil and season. When the pan is hot, place the halves cut side down and cook for 1–2 minutes over a high heat until griddle marks appear.

5. To serve, place a sweet potato hash on each plate, spoon over the frijoles, top with a fried egg and serve each with a griddled avocado half. Crumble over the feta and sprinkle with chopped coriander leaves and a little extra chilli. Serve with lime wedges.

PAN-FRIED MACKEREL, AVO & GRAPEFRUIT

*GLUTEN-FREE *DAIRY-FREE

Bittersweet grapefruit contrasts so well with rich avo and juicy succulent mackerel. This is an effortless starter that's really easy to make but bound to impress the socks off your guests.

Serves 4 as a starter or light lunch

2 pink grapefruit, reserve
  2 tablespoons juice for
  the dressing
1 fennel bulb, trimmed,
  any fronds reserved
1 ripe avocado
50g watercress
4 fresh mackerel fillets
Groundnut oil

For the dressing
2 tablespoons extra virgin
  olive oil, plus a little
  extra for the mackerel
1 tablespoon lemon juice
  or white wine vinegar
1 teaspoon Dijon mustard
1 teaspoon clear honey
Sea salt and freshly
  ground black pepper
½ red onion, finely sliced
1 red chilli, deseeded and
  finely chopped

1. Start by removing the pith and peel from the grapefruit with a serrated knife. Then cut in between the pith to release the segments and transfer to a large bowl.

2. Now make the dressing. Squeeze the grapefruit juice from the remaining pithy membranes into a jug (you only need 2 tablespoons of juice). Add the olive oil, lemon juice or vinegar, mustard and honey to the jug, whisk together and season to taste. Add the red onion and chilli.

3. Slice the fennel as thinly as you can, then add to the grapefruit segments, along with the avocado slices and watercress.

4. Preheat a dry frying pan until hot. Lightly rub the fish fillets with a little oil on both sides, then season all over. Add to the hot pan skin side down. Cook for 3 minutes over a mediun-high heat until the skin turns crisp, then flip over and cook for a further minute or until just cooked through. Remove the pan from the heat.

5. Pour the dressing over the salad and gently toss together to coat. Divide the salad between four plates and top each one with a mackerel fillet.

STEAK, CHIMICHURRI & SWEETCORN SALSA

*GLUTEN-FREE *DAIRY-FREE

Argentinian chimichurri sauce is big, bold and packs a world of flavour into one hit. Use this as a dressing for a tomato-avo-sweetcorn salsa and you've got the perfect adornment for juicy rare steak. This is delicious just as it is, but serve with sweet potato chips or a green salad alongside if you like.

Serves 4

For the salsa

½ red onion, finely chopped
1 garlic clove, finely chopped
1 red chilli, deseeded and
   finely chopped
2 tablespoons red wine
   vinegar
4 teaspoons olive oil
¼ teaspoon hot chilli powder
Sea salt and freshly ground
   black pepper
1 sweetcorn cob
1 tablespoon finely
   chopped parsley
½ teaspoon dried oregano
1 ripe avocado
125g cherry tomatoes,
   quartered

For the steak

4 ribeye or sirloin steaks
2 teaspoons olive oil

1. First make the chimichurri salsa. Put the onion, garlic, chilli and vinegar in a bowl and set aside.

2. Meanwhile, heat a griddle or frying pan until hot. Mix 1 teaspoon of the olive oil with the chilli powder and some seasoning. Rub the sweetcorn cob all over with the spiced oil. When hot, add the corn to the griddle pan and cook for 10–15 minutes, turning every couple of minutes until lightly charred and cooked through. Transfer to a board and leave to cool for a few minutes.

3. Return the pan to the heat. Brush each steak all over with ½ teaspoon of oil and season. When hot, add the steaks and fry over a high heat for 3 minutes, turn over and cook for a further 2–3 minutes. This should be medium rare, but will depend on the thickness of your steaks. Cook for longer if you prefer them less pink. Transfer to a warm plate and set aside to rest for a few minutes. You may need to cook the steak in batches depending on the size of your pan.

4. Add the parsley, oregano and remaining oil into the bowl with the salsa. On a clean board, firmly hold the cooled sweetcorn cob on its end and use a sharp knife to cut away the charred kernels. Add these to the salsa, along with the diced avocado flesh and cherry tomatoes. Toss together and season to taste.

5. Serve the steaks with the chimichurri salsa.

AVOCADO &
BACON 'NIÇOISE'

*GLUTEN-FREE *DAIRY-FREE

As a rule, a Niçoise salad is not to be messed with –
perfectly balanced as all French dishes tend to be. But
swap tuna for crisp smoked bacon and add in soft and
creamy sliced avocado and you have a twist on this
classic that deserves to be eaten.

Serves 4

500g new potatoes
200g green beans, trimmed
8–12 rashers of smoked
    streaky bacon
4 medium eggs, room
    temperature
2 little gem lettuce,
    separated into leaves
225g mini plum or
    cherry tomatoes,
    quartered lengthways
2 ripe avocados
16 black olives, pitted
    and halved

For the dressing
2 teaspoons Dijon or
    wholegrain mustard
2 teaspoons clear honey
4 tablespoons olive oil
2 tablespoons white wine
    vinegar
Sea salt and freshly
    ground black pepper

1. Preheat the grill to high. Cook
the potatoes in a large pan of
boiling salted water for about
20 minutes until tender. Add
the green beans for the last
4 minutes of the cooking time.
Then drain and run under cool
water until cold.

2. Meanwhile, arrange the bacon
on a grill rack. Grill for about
5 minutes, turning halfway until
crisp. Set aside.

3. Put the eggs into a small
saucepan and cover with cold
water. Bring to the boil, then
simmer for 3 minutes for a runny
yolk, 4 minutes for soft set yolk
or up to 5 minutes if you prefer
a harder set yolk. Drain, put the
eggs in a bowl and cover with
cold water. Then peel and cut the
eggs in half.

4. Next make the dressing by
whisking all the ingredients
together with a pinch of salt and
generous grind of black pepper.

5. Slice the cooled potatoes and
add to a large salad bowl with the
green beans, lettuce, tomatoes,
sliced avocado and olives. Then
drizzle over the dressing and
gently toss the salad. Divide
between four plates, top with the
halved eggs and crispy bacon.
Serve straight away.

Very fresh eggs are
difficult to peel. Use
eggs that are a couple
of weeks old to make
removing the shell
easier.

BLAT (BACON, LETTUCE, AVOCADO & TOMATO')

*DAIRY-FREE

Avocado gives the ultimate upgrade to this breakfast or brunch classic. Pile it high, and if you're feeling extra hungry, add a fried egg on top to really finish it off.

Serves 2

6 rashers good-quality
   smoked streaky bacon
1 firm but ripe avocado
1 tablespoon good-quality
   mayonnaise (optional)
½ lemon
Sea salt and freshly
   ground black pepper
4 thick slices of your
   favourite bread (soft white
   farmhouse loaf works well)
4 little gem lettuce leaves
   or other crisp lettuce
1 large vine ripened
   tomato, sliced
Tomato ketchup (optional),
   to serve

1. Preheat the grill to high. Arrange the bacon rashers on a grill rack. When hot, grill the bacon for about 5 minutes, turning halfway until the fat is golden and starting to crisp.

2. Peel the avocado then whizz half the flesh with the mayonnaise, if using, and a good squeeze of lemon. Add salt and freshly ground black pepper to taste. Set aside.

3. Heat a ridged, non-stick griddle pan until hot. Thickly slice the remaining avocado half. Griddle the slices for 30 seconds on each side, or until griddle marks appear.

4. Toast the bread, spread with the avocado 'mayo', then layer up with the lettuce, tomato, griddled avocado and bacon. Sandwich together with the remaining slices of toasted bread. Serve straight away, with ketchup, if you like.

When chopping avocado, some people prefer to leave the skin on to give them more grip. While holding a destoned avocado half in place, cut side up, carefully dice the avocado flesh or slice without cutting through to the skin. Then scoop out the flesh with a spoon to keep the pieces intact.

GREEN GREATNESS
SALAD *VEGETARIAN *GLUTEN-FREE *DAIRY-FREE

Eat this on its own as a virtuous, feel good lunch, or crumble over feta, add chicken, mackerel, salmon or eggs for a more filling meal.

Serves 4

175g quinoa (or about 500g
   ready cooked quinoa)
200g purple sprouting or
   tenderstem broccoli,
   cut into pieces
150g frozen edamame beans
2 tablespoons whole
   almonds, skin on
2 tablespoons mixed seeds
   (sunflower and pumpkin
   seeds work well)
100g spinach
2 ripe avocados, sliced
4 spring onions, finely sliced
A small handful each of
   parsley and mint leaves,
   roughly chopped

For the dressing
3 tablespoons extra
   virgin olive oil
4 tablespoons lemon juice
2 teaspoons clear honey
1 garlic clove, squashed
Sea salt and freshly
   ground black pepper

1. Cook the quinoa in a large pan of boiling water or gluten-free vegetable stock for 15–20 minutes, or until tender. Drain well and transfer to a large bowl.

2. Meanwhile, cook the broccoli in a pan of boiling water for 3–4 minutes until just tender, adding the edamame for the last minute of cooking time. Drain well, then add to a bowl of cold or iced water to prevent the vegetables from overcooking.

3. For the dressing, place the oil, lemon juice, honey and garlic in a clean jam jar with a pinch of salt and pepper. Secure the lid and shake well until the dressing has emulsified. Set aside.

4. Heat a dry frying pan until hot, add the almonds and cook for a couple of minutes, tossing the almonds occasionally until toasted. Set aside to cool slightly, then chop. Return the pan to the heat, add the seeds and toast for a couple of minutes. Set aside.

5. Remove the garlic clove from the dressing, then pour over the quinoa, add the cooked and cooled vegetables, spinach, sliced avocado, spring onions and herbs. Gently toss together to dress the salad. Scatter over the toasted seeds and nuts.

GREEN & CLEAN POTATO SALAD

*VEGETARIAN *GLUTEN-FREE

This is a tasty alternative to the traditional British potato salad. It is delicious in its own right, but being free from mayonnaise, this is the perfect choice for those who can't eat eggs or simply prefer a more nourishing, cleaner alternative. Serve on a sunny summer's day with roast chicken and a peppery watercress or green salad.

Serves 4

500g new potatoes
1 ripe avocado
1 teaspoon Dijon mustard
1 tablespoon lemon juice
2 tablespoons Greek yogurt
½ teaspoon honey
Sea salt and freshly
   ground black pepper
½ red onion or 4 spring
   onions, finely chopped
A small handful of
   flat leaf parsley,
   chopped

1. Cook the potatoes in a large pan of boiling, salted water for about 20 minutes until tender. Drain well, cool under cold running water, drain again and set aside.

2. Meanwhile, roughly chop half the avocado flesh and place in a food-processor along with the mustard, lemon juice, yogurt, honey and a generous pinch of salt and pepper. Whizz until smooth and season to taste.

3. Halve or quarter any large potatoes then add to a bowl. Cut the remaining avocado into chunky cubes and add to the bowl with the red (or spring) onion and parsley. Add the dressing and toss gently to coat. Serve straight away.

AVOCADO SALSA VERDE

*DAIRY-FREE

Rich nuggets of silky smooth avocado soften the salty, sour, herby punch of a traditional salsa verde in this version. It tastes delicious with barbecued lamb cutlets or roasted white fish.

Serves 4

1 garlic clove, finely
  chopped
1 tablespoon white wine
  vinegar
1 teaspoon Dijon mustard
Freshly ground black
  pepper
Pinch of sugar or
  ½ teaspoon clear honey
1 tablespoon capers in
  brine, drained and
  roughly chopped
25g cornichons, drained
  and sliced
2 anchovies in oil, drained
  and finely chopped
1 shallot, finely chopped
15g each flat-leaf parsley
  and mint leaves, roughly
  chopped
3 tablespoons extra virgin
  olive oil or avocado oil
1 large ripe avocado, cut
  into 1cm dice
Freshly grilled lamb cutlets
  or fish, to serve

1. Place the garlic in a medium sized bowl. Add the vinegar, mustard, some freshly ground black pepper and a pinch of sugar or a little honey. Whisk with a fork to combine.

2. Add the capers, cornichons and anchovies, if using, to the same bowl. Stir in the chopped shallot, chopped herbs and olive or avocado oil and mix gently to combine.

3. Mash a quarter of the avocado cubes with a fork until smooth. Stir this into the salsa, then gently mix with the remaining avocado. Serve with freshly grilled lamb cutlets or fish.

Toss prepared avocado flesh with a little lemon or lime juice to prevent discolouration.

SWEET

NUTTY CHOC-AVO SPREAD *VEGETARIAN *DAIRY-FREE *GLUTEN-FREE

Shop bought chocolate spreads are high in energy but low in nutrients. Avocado boosts the nourishing power of this homemade breakfast spread and it's also free from any nasty additives and preservatives. Make a batch for the weekend and slather onto your favourite toast. Try swapping hazelnuts for almonds or cashews. It will keep chilled, in an airtight container for up to four days.

Makes 1 × 275ml jar (about 275g)

100g blanched hazelnuts
1 ripe avocado
½ teaspoon vanilla extract
25g good-quality cocoa powder (I use Green & Blacks; check the label to ensure it is dairy-free), sifted
4 tablespoons maple syrup
Sea salt
Toast, to serve

1. Preheat the oven to 180°C/fan 160°C/gas mark 4. Spread the nuts out on a baking tray and cook for 10 minutes until toasted and golden. Leave to cool.

2. Transfer the cooled nuts to a food-processor and whizz until finely ground. Continue to whizz until they turn to a paste.

3. Roughly chop the avocado flesh and add to the food-processor along with the vanilla extract, cocoa, maple syrup and a pinch of sea salt. Whizz until smooth.

4. Transfer to a jar or airtight container and keep chilled. Spread on freshly toasted bread.

MAPLE PECAN CHOCOLATE POTS

*VEGETARIAN *DAIRY-FREE *GLUTEN-FREE

These delightfully moreish make-ahead puds feel as indulgent as a classic chocolate mousse but are made without cream, eggs or chocolate. They're surprisingly rich and chocolatey, so a little goes a long way. This recipe makes 4 small servings – it will easily double if you're feeling greedy!

Serves 4

1 large ripe avocado
1 large ripe banana, peeled and chopped
4 tablespoons maple syrup
40g good-quality cocoa powder (I use Green & Blacks; check the label to ensure it is dairy-free), sifted

For the pecan brittle
Flavourless oil for greasing, such as groundnut
50g pecans
50g caster sugar
2 tablespoons maple syrup
Sea salt

1. First make the chocolate pots. Place the avocado flesh in a food-processor with the chopped banana, maple syrup, cocoa and a small pinch of salt. Whizz until smooth.

2. Spoon into four small glasses or espresso cups and chill in the fridge for at least 1 hour or up to 6 hours ahead.

3. Meanwhile, make the maple pecan brittle. Line a baking tray with greaseproof paper and lightly grease with a little flavourless oil. Scatter the pecans onto the tray and set aside.

4. Put the sugar, maple syrup and 1 tablespoon of cold water in a heavy-based, non-stick frying pan. Heat very gently until the sugar dissolves, without stirring. This will take about 5 minutes. Then allow to bubble until it turns dark golden in colour, which will take a further 3–5 minutes. The water needs to evaporate for the sugar to turn into caramel (and set hard). Add the salt then pour the caramel over the nuts. Leave to cool for at least 30 minutes until hard. Then bash with a rolling pin to break into shards.

5. Add a few shards of pecan brittle to each chocolate pot just before serving.

COCONUT CHOCOLATE TRUFFLES

*VEGETARIAN *DAIRY-FREE *GLUTEN-FREE

These are so simple to make and omit the saturated fat-laden double cream traditionally used in a chocolate ganache. Avocado adds richness and indulgence as well as lots of goodness. Play around with the toppings – try crushed pistachios, finely chopped toasted hazelnuts or grated chocolate sprinkles.

Makes 18–20 truffles

125g good-quality dark chocolate (about 70 per cent cocoa solids; check the label to ensure it is dairy-free), chopped
2½ tablespoons light brown sugar
½ teaspoon vanilla extract
1 small ripe avocado (you need 130g flesh)
3 tablespoons coconut cream
50g desiccated coconut, for coating

1. Slowly melt the chocolate and sugar in a heatproof bowl over a saucepan of barely simmering water. Once melted, remove from the heat and stir in the vanilla extract. Leave to cool for about 20 minutes.

2. Roughly chop the avocado flesh, add to a food-processor, then add the cooled chocolate mixture and coconut cream. Whizz until smooth. Scrape into a bowl and refrigerate for at least 2 hours or until firm.

3. Spread the desiccated coconut out on a large tray. Take a teaspoonful of the mixture and roll into a ball, then roll in the coconut to coat. Repeat until you have used all the mixture, then transfer to a tray lined with greaseproof paper and chill until needed. They will keep for up to 2–3 days in an airtight container in the fridge.

PISTACHIO & AVOCADO
ICE CREAM

*VEGETARIAN *DAIRY-FREE *GLUTEN-FREE

Avocado lends itself perfectly to this twist on the Italian favourite. Its vibrant green colour goes hand in hand with the pistachio's natural hue and provides creaminess and richness without the need for dairy or eggs.

Serves 8–10
Makes 850ml

400ml can full-fat
  coconut milk
100g golden caster sugar
150g shelled pistachio
  kernels
1 medium ripe avocado
  (about 160g)
Sea salt

1. Place the coconut milk and sugar in a saucepan. Heat very gently over a low heat until the sugar dissolves – don't allow to boil. Remove from the heat. Leave to cool, then refrigerate for at least an hour until cold.

2. When the coconut mixture is completely chilled, add the pistachios to a food-processor and grind to a powder. Next, add the avocado flesh, then add the coconut mixture and a pinch of salt and blend until smooth. Taste and add a little more salt, if needed.

3. Transfer to an ice cream maker and churn for 30–40 minutes until very thick, then transfer to a freezer proof container (about 1 litre) and freeze for at least 4 hours, or until ready to use. If you don't have an ice cream maker, transfer the mixture to a freezer proof container and freeze for at least 8 hours, whisking every 30 minutes until solid.

If you have leftover ripe avocado, there's no need to throw it in the compost; you can freeze it. The texture of the thawed avocado won't be nice in salads, but is perfect for whizzing into smoothies and dressings or smashing into guacamole.

SQUIDGY CHOCOLATE HAZELNUT BROWNIES

*VEGETARIAN *DAIRY-FREE

Unctuous, squidgy and super chocolatey, these brownies taste anything but healthy. I won't pretend they are completely virtuous, but using avocado instead of butter reduces the saturated fat content (and overall calories), making these brownies less guilt inducing than the traditional variety. It also makes them a winner for anyone who is lactose intolerant. Share them with friends or family alongside a big pot of tea.

Serves 12–16

100g blanched hazelnuts

150g good-quality dark chocolate (about 70 per cent cocoa solids; check it's dairy-free), chopped

50g coconut oil, plus extra for greasing

3 medium eggs

200g light muscovado sugar

1 teaspoon vanilla extract

1 medium-large ripe avocado (about 175g flesh)

100g self-raising flour

25g good-quality cocoa powder (check it's dairy-free)

Sea salt

1. Preheat the oven to 180°C/fan 160°C/gas mark 4. Grease and line a 20cm square brownie tin with greaseproof paper. Spread the hazelnuts out in a large roasting tin and bake for 6–8 minutes until toasted. Set aside to cool then roughly chop. Melt 100g of chocolate and the coconut oil in a heatproof bowl over a saucepan of barely simmering water, remove from the heat and leave to cool slightly.

2. Meanwhile, whizz together the eggs, sugar and vanilla in a food-processor until combined. Add the avocado flesh and process until smooth. Transfer to a large bowl, add the cooled chocolate mixture, sift in the flour and cocoa, add a pinch of salt, then whisk everything together. Fold in most of the chopped hazelnuts and the remaining chocolate.

3. Spoon into the brownie tin and level. Scatter over the remaining chopped hazelnuts. Bake for 20–25 minutes until just firm to the touch. Cool slightly in the tin before transferring to a wire rack to cool completely. Cut into squares. These are also delicious served warm with vanilla ice cream for dessert, if you can eat dairy. The cooled brownies will keep in an airtight container for up to 3 days.

If you like mocha brownies add 2 teaspoons of instant espresso powder and swap the chunks for milk chocolate, if you eat dairy.

BANANA & WALNUT BREAD *VEGETARIAN *DAIRY-FREE

Avocado is swapped in again for butter to make this a naturally dairy-free cake. It also makes it much lower in saturated fat and lower in calories than regular banana cakes. Use ripe or overripe bananas for this recipe. Whenever you are left with a speckled-skinned banana that is too ripe to eat, freeze it in its skin, and defrost before using.

Serves 10

75g walnuts, roughly chopped
½ medium ripe avocado (about 75g flesh)
125g light muscovado sugar
1 large egg
1 teaspoon vanilla extract
175g plain flour
2 teaspoons baking powder
Sea salt
3 ripe or overripe bananas (about 275–300g), roughly mashed

1. Preheat the oven to 180°C/fan 160°C/gas mark 4. Line a non-stick 900g (2lb) loaf tin (21cm × 10cm × 7cm) with greaseproof paper. You can lightly grease with coconut oil if not using a non-stick tin.

2. Spread the walnuts out on a baking tray and bake for 5 minutes. Leave to cool, then roughly chop.

3. Meanwhile, put the avocado flesh, sugar, egg and vanilla extract into a food-processor. Whiz until smooth. Transfer to a large bowl.

4. Sift over the flour, baking powder and a pinch of salt. Whisk until combined, then whisk in most of the banana until smooth. Fold in the remaining banana and most of the toasted walnuts. Spoon into the prepared tin, scatter with the rest of the walnuts and place on a baking tray.

5. Bake for about 1 hour, or until a skewer inserted into the middle comes out clean. You may need to return it to the oven for 5–10 minutes if it still seems a bit sticky in the centre. Leave to cool in the tin for 15 minutes before transferring to a cooling rack to cool completely. The cake will keep in an airtight container for 3–4 days.

EQUIPMENT: THE ESSENTIALS

More often than not, there's little more than a fork or a decent, sharp cook's knife needed, but there are one or two other bits of basic equipment you might find useful.

Pestle and mortar

This is very useful for crushing garlic or spices and smashing small amounts of avocado.

A decent box grater

Ideal for grating raw carrots, beetroot or courgettes into salads and slaws. A spiraliser is great if you have the storage space, but a grater or julienne peeler does the same thing; it just takes a little more time and patience.

A fine grater

This is one of my most-used utensils, excellent for speedily grating fresh garlic and root ginger as well as cheese. I use a Microplane but there are plenty of good brands available.

A simple citrus reamer or juicer

Limes and lemons are an avocado's best friend and used in many recipes. You don't need any fancy gadgetry here, just something to help you efficiently extract juice and separate the pips.

Mini food-processor

This is one gadget I couldn't live without. It is brilliant for making chunky purées, guacamole, pastes and whizzing into dressings. It is also great for speedily chopping onions and garlic. If you don't have one, a pestle and mortar can be used for purées and pastes, but if you spend a lot of time in the kitchen, it is a worthwhile (and affordable) investment. A handheld stick blender is also a good alternative.

Food-processor

Larger than its mini sibling (above), this is so useful for making larger quantities of guacamole or hummus. I also use it for whizzing cake mixture or making nut butter, ganache or an ice cream base. It can also be used for soups and smoothies if you don't have a blender. It often comes with lots of useful attachments, including graters, juicers, dough hooks and a smaller bowl.

High speed blender/ smoothie maker or nutri bullet

This is not an essential, but with a super sharp blade and extra power, it is excellent for giving a velvety smooth finish to soups and smoothies. A good investment if you make smoothies regularly.

Digital scales

In the savoury recipes in this book, a guide is given for the size of the avocado needed, but a few grams here or there won't make much difference. For baking, however, I like to be more precise, and a set of digital scales will give you accuracy and peace of mind, which can make all the difference to your finished bake.

USEFUL NOTES
ON INGREDIENTS

How to freeze leftover avocado
There are two main ways to freeze avocado:

♦ Hass avocados were used in the testing of these recipes as these are the most widely available variety, but it should be interchangeable with other varieties.

♦ All **vegetables, herbs and salad** ingredients are washed.

♦ **Garlic, onion and shallots** are peeled, unless stated otherwise.

♦ **Lemons and limes** – these vary in their juiciness, so use the amounts stated in the recipes as a general guide and add more juice to taste.

♦ **Chillies** – the heat in chillies can vary, so it's important to use these recipes as a guide and adjust to your taste, leaving in the seeds if you prefer a more intense heat level. You can always add more to boost the heat, but it's much harder to take it away!

♦ **Sea salt** – I prefer to use a natural sea or rock salt for a better flavour. Fine table salt often contains anti-caking agents to prevent the crystals from sticking together.

♦ **Meat, fish and eggs** – buy the best you can afford, ideally they should be sustainably sourced and free range.

♦ **Seasoning** – this is very much down to personal taste, so I have only specified an amount of salt where I think it is essential to a recipe. For the rest of the recipes, add as much or as little as you like to suit your palette.

As a purée: whizz in a mini food-processor with a little lemon or lime juice, then transfer to a freezer bag and label, or fill up ice cube trays.
As halves: halve, stone and peel the avocado, sprinkle with a little lemon juice, wrap tightly in clingfilm, then place in a freezer bag, seal and freeze. Defrost before using. Defrost before using in smoothies, dressings or dips.

Weights and measures
All teaspoon and tablespoon measures are level.
All avocados are halved, stoned and peeled before use.
Average weight of an avocado (flesh only):
Large = 200g
Medium = 150–175g
Small = 125g

INDEX

ACKNOWLEDGEMENTS

Heaps of ideas, countless tests, masses of photographs and possibly hundreds of avocados later and the book is complete, well, almost. First, there are a few very important thank yous to be said.

My first big thank you has to be to Kyle for giving me the opportunity to write my début cookbook. I'm so grateful to have had the chance to write 40 recipes using an ingredient which I genuinely ADORE. I've loved every part of the process, so thank you.

I'd also like to say a big thank you to the rest of the team at Kyle Books; I really do appreciate all of the hard work that goes on behind the scenes; your attention to detail and quest for perfection is second to none. In particular to Vicky, for initially helping me turn the idea into a reality, and to Claire for your patience, advice and support throughout. And a big thank you to Helen for sprinkling your design magic and sewing the chapters together so beautifully.

I'm incredibly lucky to have worked with such a fantastic and talented team – a great deal of hard work went into the photoshoots, so I owe special thanks to all of those who made these days a joy as well as a success.

To Clare – what can I say? Your beautiful photography is an inspiration, and I am in total awe of how you make such a skill appear so effortless. I've so enjoyed our shoots; your 'nothing is too much trouble' attitude, unshakeable composure and sense of humour were invaluable.

Wei, thank you for bringing your unique touch and unquashable enthusiasm to this project. Your fabulous props are always just right – and, as always, you are so lovely to work with.

Jenna, thank you for loving avocados as much as I do, and for all your hard work. You are a wonderful cook.

Finally, to my family, for your love, unwavering support and interest in all of my work. This means the world to me. And lastly, but by no means least, to Ian for putting up with my avocado 'tunnel vision' for a good few months and for remaining excited about your fifth avocado-based meal of a weekend. Thank you for your honesty and exacting tastebuds, but, most of all, thank you for challenging, inspiring and believing in me.

First published in Great Britain in 2016 by
Kyle Books, an imprint of Kyle Cathie Ltd
192–198 Vauxhall Bridge Road
London SW1V 1DX
general.enquiries@kylebooks.com
www.kylebooks.co.uk

10 9 8 7 6 5 4 3 2 1

ISBN 978 0 85783 378 5

Project Editor: Claire Rogers
Copy Editor: Eve Pertile
Designer: Helen Bratby
Photographer: Clare Winfield
Illustrator: Jenni Desmond
Food Stylist: Lucy Jessop
Food Stylist's Assistant: Jenna Leiter
Prop Stylist: Wei Tang
Production: Nic Jones and Gemma John

A Cataloguing in Publication record
for this title is available from the British
Library.

Colour reproduction by ALTA London
Printed and bound in China by C&C Offset
Printing Co., Ltd.

* Note: all eggs are free-range